www.FlowerpotPress.com
PAB-0808-0186 · 978-1-4867-1574-9
Made in China/Fabriqué en Chine

# FINN'S FUN TRUCKS
# THE CONSTRUCTION CREW

Written by Finn Coyle  Illustrated by Srimalie Bassani

We are the construction crew. We build things with the help of some really awesome trucks.

Each one has a job of its own.
Can you guess what each one does?

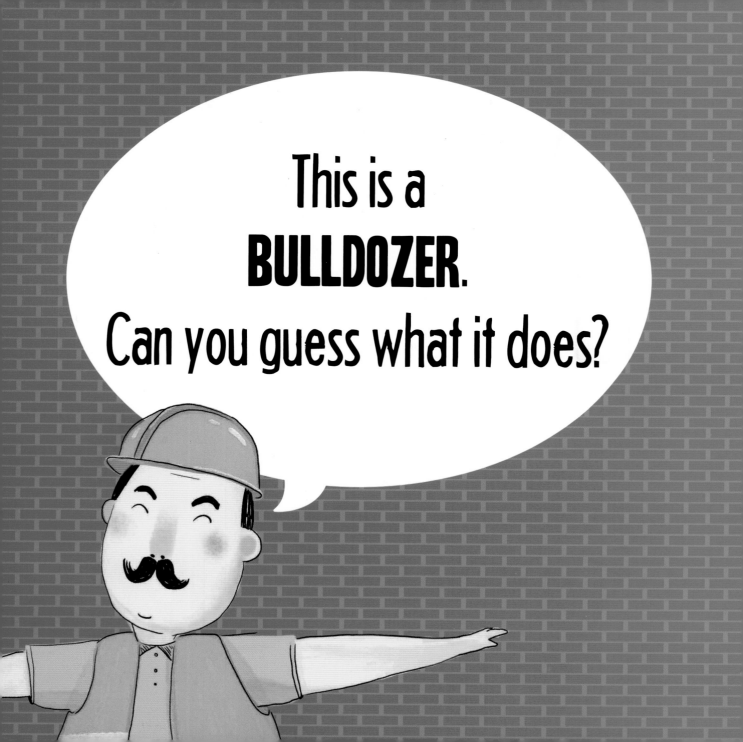

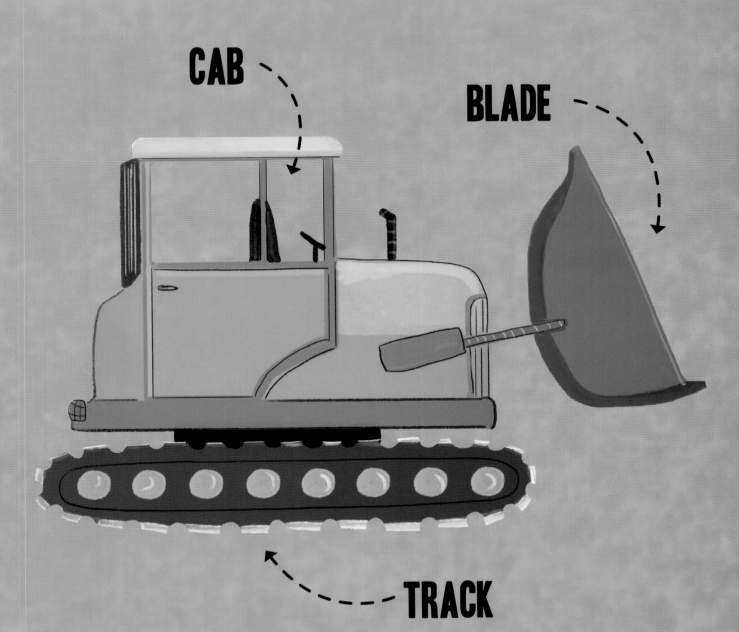

CAB

BLADE

TRACK

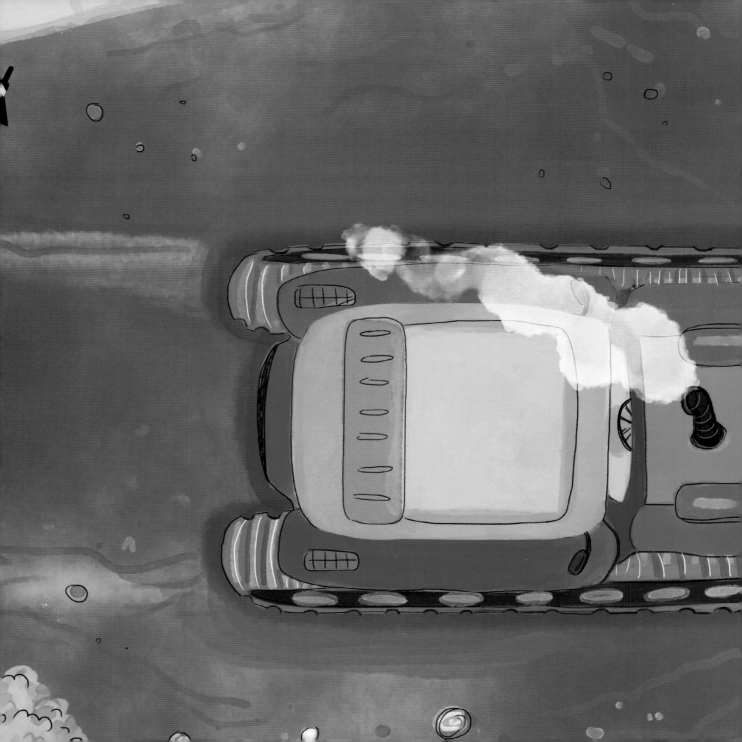

The bulldozer pushes dirt around and flattens the ground to make room for new buildings.

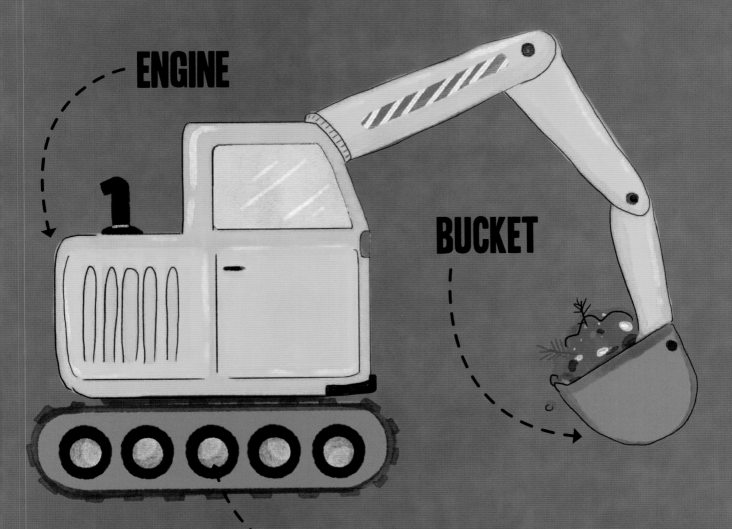

ENGINE

BUCKET

SPROCKET

The excavator digs into the ground to remove dirt and soil. It can also move dirt around the worksite.

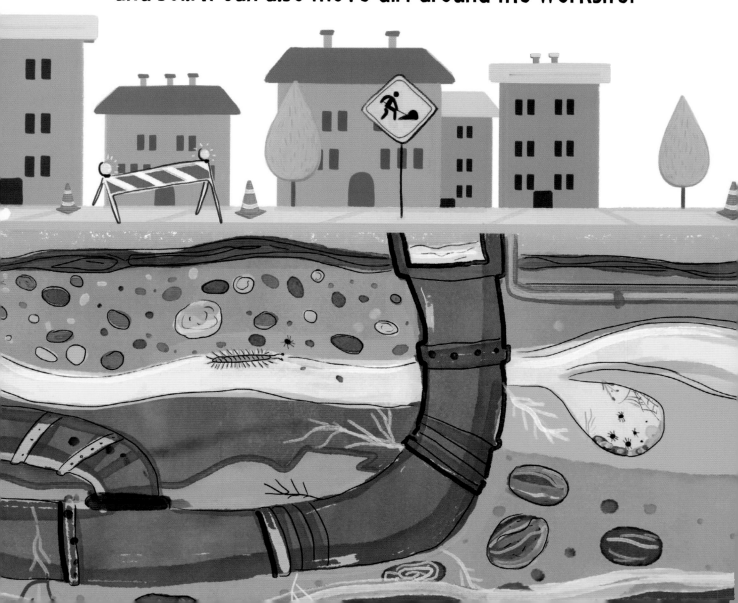

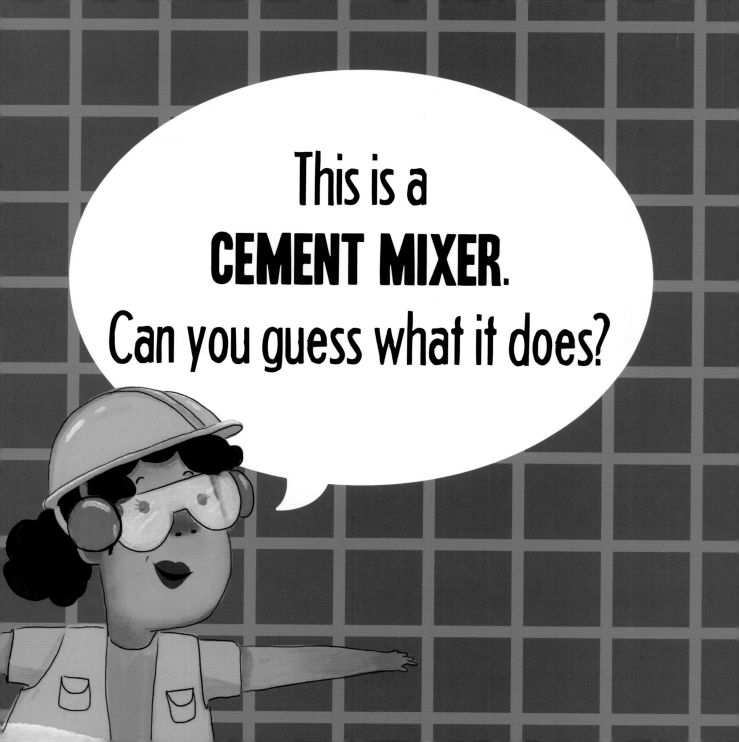

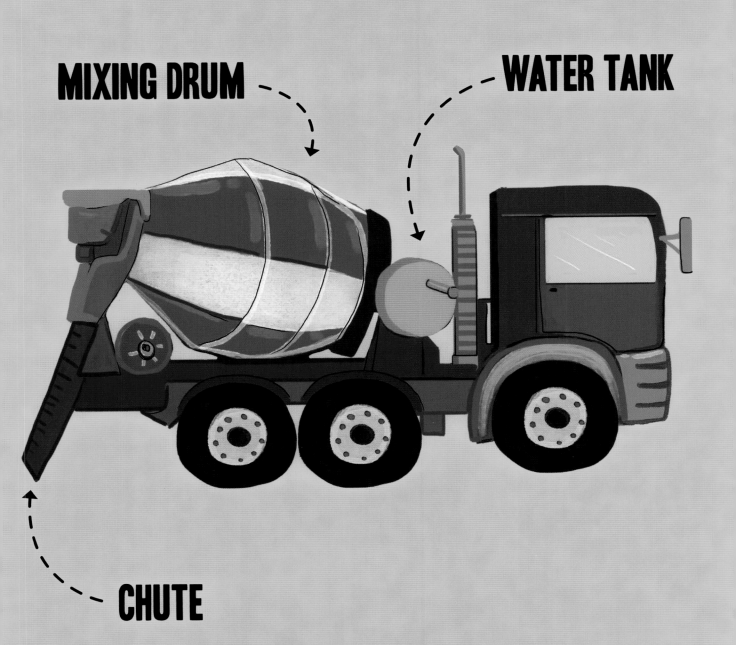

The cement mixer mixes up cement and pours it out at the worksite to lay a foundation.

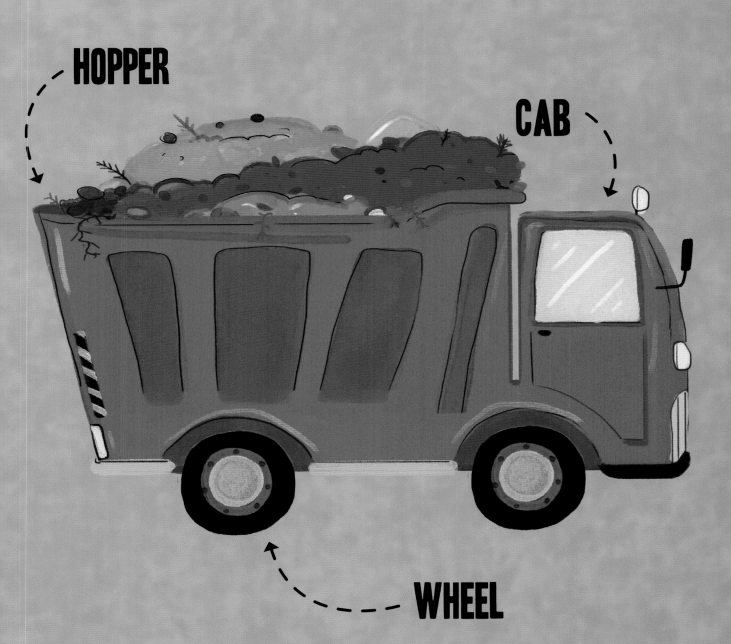

HOPPER

CAB

WHEEL

The dump truck carries big, heavy loads and moves them into and out of the worksite.

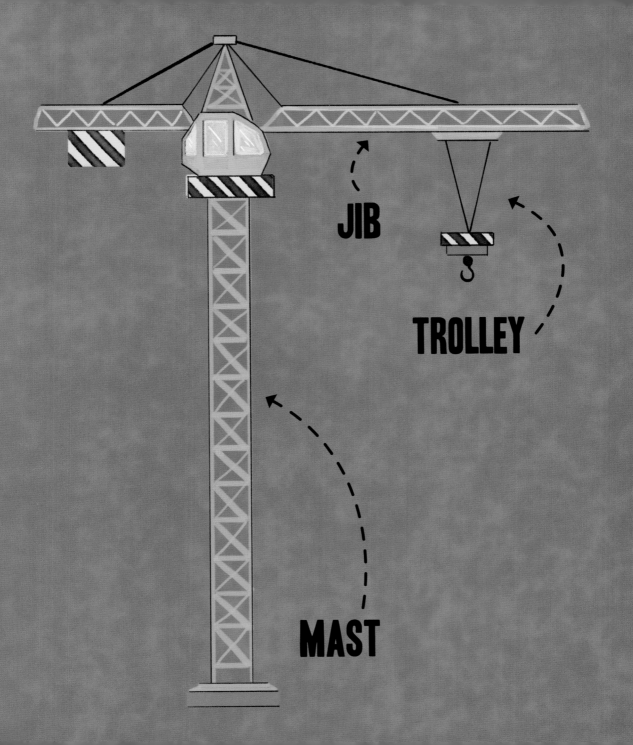

JIB

TROLLEY

MAST

The tower crane picks up heavy loads and moves them around, sometimes to the tops of tall buildings.

Can you guess what we can do
when we all work together?

We can build brand new buildings in our city!

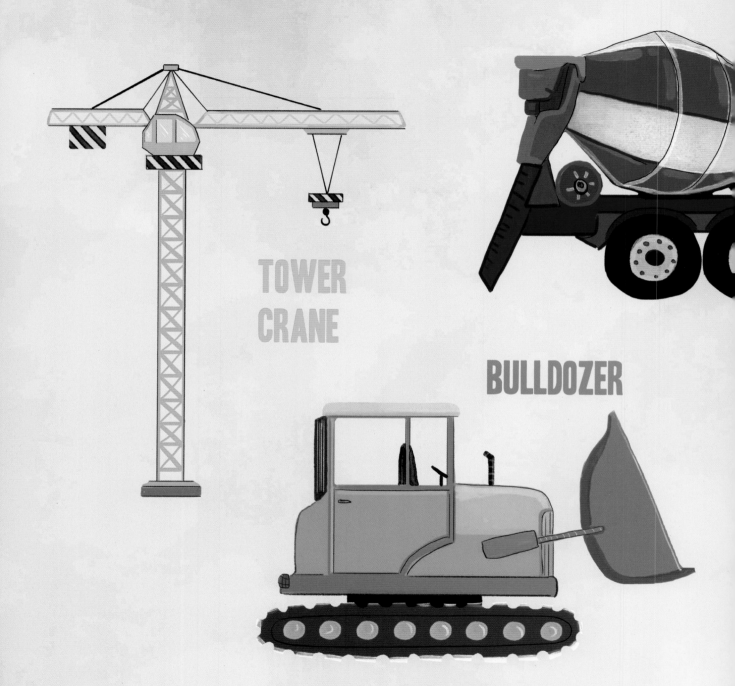

TOWER
CRANE

BULLDOZER

**A** IS FOR **ADAM**, THE FIRST MAN.

 **B** IS FOR **BIBLE**, GOD'S HOLY WORD.

## God Created

Genesis 1:1 // Words & music by Stephen Elkins

### Chorus

In the beginning! Oh, in the beginning!
In the beginning, Oh, in the beginning!
In the beginning! Oh, in the beginning!
In the beginning, Oh, in the beginning!

In the beginning
God created the heavens and the earth.
In the beginning,
God created the heavens and the earth,
In the beginning
God created the heavens and the earth.
In the beginning
God created the heavens and the earth.

**C** is for CREATION.

**GOD MADE EVERYTHING.** When God said,
"Let there be light," there was light! He called the light
day, and the dark night. That is what God did on the first
day. On the second day, God made the sky. On the third
day, he made the mountains and oceans.
Then He made the trees and flowers.
On the fourth day, God made the sun, moon, and stars.
On the fifth day, God filled the oceans and lakes with fish.
He made the birds and butterflies too. On the sixth day,
God made all the animals. He made people, too.

**D** IS FOR **DANIEL**. HE SLEPT WITH LIONS!

**E** IS FOR **EZEKIEL**, WHO DREAMED OF DRY BONES.

## Peter, James, and John in a Sailboat

Peter, James, and John in a sailboat
Peter, James, and John in a sailboat
Peter, James, and John in a sailboat
Out on the deep blue sea.

They fished all night and they caught no fishes
Fished all night and they caught no fishes
Fished all night and they caught no fishes
Out on the deep blue sea.

A lesson they heard from the Savior:
"I will make you fishers of men."
Oh, what a glorious Savior,
A wonderful teacher and friend

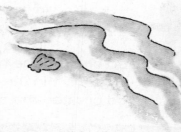

Peter, James, and John in a sailboat
Peter, James, and John in a sailboat
Peter, James, and John in a sailboat
Out on the deep blue sea.
Out on the deep blue sea.

**F** is for FISHERMEN.

JESUS WANTED SOME HELPERS. One day Jesus was walking beside
the Sea of Galilee. He saw some fishermen working. Peter and Andrew were
in a boat fishing. James and John were mending their nets.
Jesus called to them, "Come, follow me. I will make you fishers of men."
At once, they left their boats to follow Jesus. They were the first disciples.
They would tell others about him.

2

# Only a Boy Named David

Only a boy named David
Only a little sling
Only a boy named David
But he could pray and sing
Only a boy named David
Only a rippling brook
Only a boy named David
But five little stones he took

And one little stone went into the sling
And the sling went 'round and 'round
And one little stone went into the sling
And the sling went 'round and 'round
And 'round and 'round and 'round and
'round and 'round and 'round and 'round
And one little stone went up in the air
And the giant came tumbling down

Ⓖ is for GOLIATH.

ONCE A GIANT NAMED GOLIATH STOOD BEFORE ISRAEL'S ARMY.
"Come and fight me!" he shouted. But everyone was afraid.
Goliath said bad things about God.
Hearing this, David took his slingshot and said, "The Lord will help me."
With one little stone, David killed the mighty giant. God did help David!

**H** IS FOR **HANNAH**, WHO PRAYED AND PRAYED.

**I** IS FOR **ISAIAH**, A GREAT PROPHET OF GOD.

## Jesus Loves Me

Jesus loves me, this I know
For the Bible tells me so
Little ones to Him belong
They are weak but He is strong

Chorus
Yes, Jesus loves me
Yes, Jesus loves me
Yes, Jesus loves me
The Bible tells me so

Jesus loves me, He who died
Heaven's gate to open wide
He will wash away my sin
Let His little child come in

Repeat chorus

Jesus loves me, He will stay
Close beside me all the way
Thou hast bled and died for me
I will henceforth live for Thee

Repeat chorus

 **J** is for JESUS.

JESUS PROMISES TO LOVE ME NO MATTER WHAT.
He loves me when I'm good. He loves me when I'm not so good.
He loves me if I win or lose.
No matter what I say or do, Jesus loves me.

**K** IS FOR **KING**. JESUS IS KING OF KINGS!

**L** IS FOR **LAMB**. JESUS IS THE LAMB OF GOD.

## He's Got the Whole World in His Hands

He's got the whole world in His hands
He's got the whole world in His hands
He's got the whole world in His hands
He's got the whole world in His hands

He's got the little bitty baby in His hands
He's got the little bitty baby in His hands
He's got the little bitty baby in His hands
He's got the whole world in His hands

He's got you and me, brother, in His hands
He's got you and me, brother, in His hands
He's got you and me, brother, in His hands
He's got the whole world in His hands

He's got you and me, sister, in His hands
He's got you and me, sister, in His hands
He's got you and me, sister, in His hands
He's got the whole world in His hands

**M** is for MOSES.

THE KING WAS SO MEAN, he was going to hurt the Jewish boy babies.
One mother wanted to hide her baby. So she made a special basket that would
float in the water. Carefully, she put her baby boy into the basket.
She set it in the river among the tall grass.
An Egyptian princess saw the basket floating in the water. When she found
the baby boy, she loved him. The princess decided to keep the baby.
She named him Moses. God took care of baby Moses.

**N** IS FOR **NOAH**, WHO BUILT AN ARK.

**O** IS FOR **ONE**. THERE IS ONLY ONE GOD.

**P** IS FOR **PETER**, WHO WALKED ON WATER.

**Q** IS FOR **QUEEN**. ESTHER BECAME A QUEEN.

# Rainbows
### Words & music by Stephen Elkins

I have set My rainbow in the clouds
And it will be a sign, a colorful sign
I have set My rainbow in the sky
A promise I make to you, here's why
Never again will waters rise
For I have set My rainbow in the sky

**R** is for RAINBOW.

IT RAINED FOR 40 DAYS AND NIGHTS.
Noah, his family, and all the animals were safe in the ark. The rain stopped.
When the land dried up, Noah, his family, and all the animals came out of the ark.
Noah thanked God for keeping them safe. God put a beautiful rainbow in the sky
to show He would never again flood the whole earth.
It was a beautiful day!

## S is for STAR.

THE THREE WISE MEN HAD SEEN A LOT OF STARS.
But they had never seen a special star like this one! This star was
moving across the eastern sky. And night after night they followed it.
Why were they following this star?
They knew God was guiding them to a new King.
The journey was long. But finally the star stopped and came
to rest over Bethlehem. Beneath the star they found the baby Jesus.
When they saw him, they bowed down and worshiped him.

## Behold That Star

**Chorus**
Behold that star,
behold that star up yonder
Behold that star,
it is the star of Bethlehem
**Repeat**

There was no room found in the inn
It is the star of Bethlehem
For Him who was born free from sin
It is the star of Bethlehem, O . . .

**Repeat chorus**

The wise men traveled from the East
It is the star of Bethlehem
To worship Him, the Prince of Peace
It is the star of Bethlehem, O . . .

**Repeat chorus**

A song broke forth upon the night
It is the star of Bethlehem
From angel hosts all robed in white
It is the star of Bethlehem, O . . .

**Repeat chorus**

**T** IS FOR THE **TEN COMMANDMENTS** GOD GAVE TO MOSES.

**U** IS FOR THE **UNIVERSE** GOD MADE.

**V** IS FOR THE **VICTORY** WE HAVE IN JESUS.

## W is for WHALE.

GOD TOLD JONAH TO SERVE HIM. But Jonah ran away and got on a ship.
While he was sailing, a storm came up. Jonah was thrown overboard.
Down he went until "Gulp!" He was swallowed by a great fish.
Jonah prayed, "I'm sorry, Lord." God saved Jonah.
Soon Jonah was serving God!

### Who Did Swallow Jonah?

Who did, who did, who did, who did
Who did swallow Jo, Jo, Jo, Jo
Who did, who did, who did, who did
Who did swallow Jo, Jo, Jo, Jo
Who did, who did, who did, who did
Who did swallow Jo, Jo, Jo, Jo
Who did swallow Jonah,
who did swallow Jonah
Who did swallow Jonah down?

Whale did, whale did, whale did, whale did
Whale did swallow Jo, Jo, Jo, Jo
(repeat 3 times)

Whale did swallow Jonah,

whale did swallow Jonah
Whale did swallow Jonah down

Gabriel, Gabriel, Gabriel, Gabriel
Gabriel blow your trum, trum, trum, trum
(repeat 3 times)
Gabriel blow your trumpet,
Gabriel blow your trumpet
Gabriel blow your trumpet loud

Noah, Noah, Noah, Noah
Noah in the arky, arky
(repeat 3 times)
Noah in the arky, Noah in the arky
Noah in the arky bailed

X IS FOR **XERXES**, WHO WAS A KING.

Y IS FOR **YAHWEH**. THAT IS GOD'S NAME!

Z IS FOR **ZACCHAEUS**, WHO CLIMBED A TREE TO SEE JESUS.

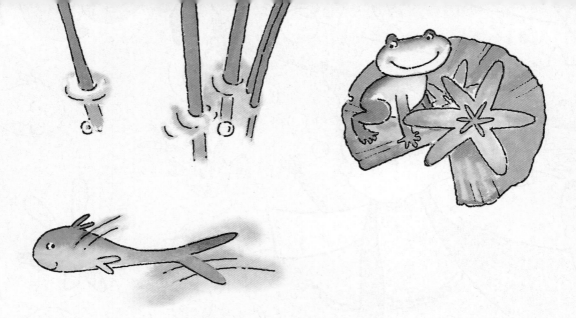

Visit Tyndale online at www.tyndale.com.

Check out Wonder Kids at http://mywonderkids.com.

*TYNDALE* and Tyndale's quill logo are registered trademarks of Tyndale House Publishers, Inc.

*Wonder Kids* is a registered trademark of The Stephens Group, Inc., DBA Wonder Workshop.

*My Book of Bible ABCs*

Copyright © 2015 by Stephen Elkins. All rights reserved.

Text adapted from Special Times Stories, copyright © 2003 by Stephen Elkins.

Artwork by Susan Reagan, orginial copyright © 2003 by Broadman and Holman. All rights released to Stephen Elkins in 2008.

All songs (except those in the public domain) written and arranged by Stephen Elkins, copyright © by Wonder Workshop, Inc., Nashville, TN. All rights reserved. Unauthorized duplication prohibited by law and the Eighth Commandment.

Designed by Jennifer Ghionzoli and Mariko Toyama.

For manufacturing information regarding this product, please call 1-800-323-9400.

ISBN 978-1-4143-9932-4

Printed in China

| 21 | 20 | 19 | 18 | 17 | 16 | 15 |
|----|----|----|----|----|----|----|
| 7  | 6  | 5  | 4  | 3  | 2  | 1  |